DUCT-TAPED
ROSES

DUCT-TAPED ROSES

POEMS

Billeh Nickerson

Book*hug Press

Toronto 2021

In loving memory of my father
William Clifford Nickerson III
March 3, 1950 to January 29, 2017

and in praise of all the Jennys

FIRST EDITION

Library and Archives Canada Cataloguing in Publication

Title: Duct-taped roses / Billeh Nickerson.

Names: Nickerson, Billeh, 1972– author.

Description: Poems.

Identifiers: Canadiana (print) 20210150238 | Canadiana (ebook) 20210150270

ISBN 9781771666909 (softcover)

ISBN 9781771666916 (EPUB)

ISBN 9781771666923 (PDF)

Classification: LCC PS8577.I32 D83 2021 | DDC C811/.6—dc23

PRINTED IN CANADA

The production of this book was made possible through the generous assistance of the Canada Council for the Arts and the Ontario Arts Council. Book*hug Press also acknowledges the support of the Government of Canada through the Canada Book Fund and the Government of Ontario through the Ontario Book Publishing Tax Credit and the Ontario Book Fund.

Book*hug Press acknowledges that the land on which we operate is the traditional territory of many nations, including the Mississaugas of the Credit, the Anishnabeg, the Chippewa, the Haudenosaunee and the Wendat peoples. We recognize the enduring presence of many diverse First Nations, Inuit and Métis peoples and are grateful for the opportunity to meet and work on this territory.

Book*hug Press

Contents

Mermen 9

Rhymes with Boyfriend 11
Six Years On 13
Pretty in Love 16
Leather Bar 18
Pickle Farmers 21
Kissing in New Zealand 23
Cheam Curling Club Circa 1988 24
Occupational Therapies 27
Hachey 30
Polkaroo 32
Zaccheus 33
Great Pyramids 35
Love Coward or What Happened after My Poem
"Driving in Adam's Jeep" Appeared on Poetry in Transit 38
Anonymous 40
1.5 Times Normal 42

Skies 43

A Baker's Dozen 57

13 Vancouver Food (in)Securities 57

Langley 67

After Joe Brainard 67

Curiosa 73

V4G 1N4 75

I've Got a Secret 76

Ball Twins 78

Let Them Eat Snake 79

To Friends Who've Worked in Porn 80

Hashtags 81

The Taxidermist 82

Sea Turtles 83

Surrealism 84

How to Clean a Gravestone 85

Acknowledgements 87

About the Author 89

Mermen

When we wrap our legs
around one another's
I'm not sure

whose limbs
are whose—
whether we're growing

fish tails
or more
entangled.

Our ocean runs deep
with possibility
but also sorrow.

Rhymes with Boyfriend

Six Years On

At my neighbourhood coffee shop,
wedged between exchange students
and scenesters with strollers,
I realize if I had conceived a child
with my best friend on the day he died
she'd start kindergarten this September.

We used to joke we'd adopt
or ask one of the Jennys to surrogate.
Jen or Jenn or Jenny, so many Jennifers
I've contemplated collective nouns—
a picnic basket of Jennys,
a jackhammer of Jennys,
an orchestra of Jennys—
for those who'd talk to our daughter
about menstruation, training bras, her changing body.

I've often discussed the loss
of mentor figures for gay men,
how those who would have taught us
what it meant to be a fortysomething
never made it that far,
but I've rarely spoken about the void
felt by a middle-aged man who loses
his gay best friend
to an accident in a bathtub.

The day we cleaned out his apartment
I looked for additional rooms,
secret passageways filled with his stuff.
The women held up his shirts
and inhaled him, but no matter how hard I tried
I couldn't resurrect his scent.

Friends ask if I expect to find him
hidden somewhere, but it's more
about my shock that he's been reduced
to things that aren't enough
to capture all he means.

In this photograph
he's mysterious,
lanky and shirtless
as he plays his vinyl
of Liz Phair's "Fuck and Run."

In this photograph
he takes off his shoes
to make sock puppets
for a karaoke version
of the theme song
from *The Muppet Show*.

In this photograph
he holds up the chinchilla
he named Hat.

In this photograph
my hands rest
on his hips,
my thumbs
along his pelvis.

In this photograph
I ask him
what the tooth fairy paid
after his childhood dentist
extracted a row of extra teeth.

In this photograph
he spells out a long word
on our whisky-stained
Scrabble board.

In this photograph
we're in the emergency room
and he's about to tell a woman
whose breast implant ruptured
that he cut himself
slicing a bagel.

In this photograph
we've convinced
tourists from Seattle
that Canadians celebrate Pride
by pulling out their cocks
to make penis flowers
on tabletops.

In this photograph
I try to recreate
his recipe
for shepherd's pie.

In this photograph,
the first day of school,
I can't find
our daughter
and I can't find him.

Pretty in Love

Envy will hurt itself
Let yourself be beautiful
Sparkling love, flowers
And pearls and pretty girls
— Frankie Goes to Hollywood, "The Power of Love"

Pretty in love with you back then
meant waking in the same position
we'd fall asleep in.
I was twenty-three or twenty-four
and you twenty-two with cheekbones
worthy of Aphrodite herself,
though my love transcended the carnal
and the pictures of you modelling
in the magazines that filled my bookshelf—
Envy will hurt itself

trying to understand how much
I've craved your embrace,
how in these twenty years
I've damned every continent
you've lived on away from me.
I have no doubt your life has been bountiful,
filled with men who have loved you
and men you have loved,
though I hope you were able to be truthful,
Let yourself be beautiful

in the face of the demons that plague
boys who grow up misunderstood
for being as much sugar and spice
as snakes and snails and puppy dog tails.
Or cocaine rails. Or champagne pain.
How many friends of ours
have we lost to the bottle, the lines, the need
to live full throttle, non-stop never-stop?
Here's my hoped-for superpower:
Sparkling love, flowers

in full bloom on command, room after room—
just like the actress, now sober,
who calculated what she once spent daily
on cocaine and filled her house each day
with roses in that amount.
You are on the other side of the world
waking without me, and I'm still pretty
in love with the memory of our joy glistening
pretty boys and pearls
and pearls and pretty girls.

Leather Bar

There's a giant wicker basket
filled with sex toys

and small bottles of wine
that make me blush

once I figure out
they're big bottles of lube.

Onstage a leather daddy
announces ticket numbers

he's commanded his submissive
to retrieve from a plastic beer jug

but whether out of apathy
or the sad fact

chaps lack pockets
no one claims the prize.

000674, anyone? Anyone?
Going once
Going twice
Last call for 000674...

Between numbers I ask
Mister Seattle Leather Daddy

if he's envious his partner
Mister Leather Washington State

is a whole state
while he's only a city

and he growls
No, because he's MINE.

000587, anyone? Anyone?
Going once
Going twice
Last call for 000587...
000655, any-one? Any-one?
Going once?

Going twice?

Last call for 000655.

After the fifteenth ticket
the leather daddy

grows increasingly annoyed
and I worry for the safety

of his submissive—
even if he consents—

as he'll surely be punished
for picking such bad numbers

but then someone screams
maybe we should all share

the sex toys and lube
amongst ourselves,

that way everyone wins
again and again and again

and apart from the two old guys
who fight over the wicker basket

everyone agrees it's the best
leather bar raffle ever.

Pickle Farmers

I was walking down the street
when a stranger in a passing truck

screamed out
Hey, pickle farmer!

which surprised me
as I wasn't wearing my gumboots

or overalls, none of my usual
pickle farmer paraphernalia.

It always surprises me
when folks who don't farm pickles

feel the need to identify me
as someone who does.

I mean, nobody screams out
Hey, dentist! or Hey, butcher!

It's not as though we're special—
a lot of people farm pickles,

some of them occasionally
some of them secretly,

like after a baseball game
their team has lost

and they think to themselves
I'm pickle-farming curious

as they stumble to the pickle field
to cultivate a few of their own.

Me, I'm more than a farmer,
I'm a pickle whisperer

who helps my fellow farmers
overcome pickle-related dilemmas

like this one farmer who loves
stuffing jars with pickles

though he often struggles
with the last one

so I whisper Just relax, *breathe easy,
and that pickle will slide right in.*

That guy in the passing truck's
just jealous of my well-kept field.

He will deny it for a while
but eventually stumble

down to the pickle field
and I'll be there to greet him.

Kissing in New Zealand

is the same as kissing
anywhere else—
your tongue doesn't
circle in the opposite direction
and you still oscillate
between not knowing
whether to open
or close your eyes—

but I needed to experience this myself,
not just read it
in some travel guide,
so when my travelling companion
went on a *Lord of the Rings* tour
I slipped into a sex club.

Who wants to fly for fourteen hours
into another hemisphere
without kissing someone there?
I guess I'm old-fashioned that way,
though I should be more specific
in my desires

as the first guy I kissed
hailed from Saskatchewan—
which is like travelling
halfway around the world
only to find yourself
eating at McDonald's.
Like good Canadians
we apologized
then moved on to find Kiwis.

Cheam Curling Club Circa 1988

In retrospect the curling club
seemed much farther away
than the forty-five-minute drive

from my home
to the army base
named for the Cheam Nation

though no one mentioned this
nor the unceded lands
just the curling

and how nice it was
for service members
to have something

to occupy their time
when not busy
defending our country.

As our bonspiel took place
on government property
our welcome bags

included not only the usual
maps and two-for-one
restaurant coupons

but personalized envelopes
with solitary
condoms

that drew screams
of laughter
from the older curlers

and silence
from me
as I'd heard about condoms

stumbled upon them
in the playgrounds
of my youth

but I hadn't touched one
or owned one
so publicly.

At some point
a drunken curler
threatened

to roll his condom
down the handle
of his curling broom

which made me think
about my friend whose mom
had her roll a condom

onto a hot dog
that for some reason
I imagined

as boiled
but it must have been fresh
from the fridge

still slippery
in her young
mortified fingers.

I recall little else
from that bonspiel
other than it took place

in Grade 8.
I'm not sure if we won
or lost.

Occupational Therapies

The Dancer

His feet were an extra pair of hands,
so even though it was the two of us
it felt like a threesome.

I wanted to be more responsive,
wanted to be more
than a giant starfish.

The Dart Player

Never have I encountered someone
so centred on the task at hand.

He'd do this thing where his pinky
would jut out to the side
just before he shot.

The Candlestick Maker

I don't remember his hands.
He smelled of vanilla.

Hachey

In memory of Aaron Hachey

In French *hache* means axe,
which may explain our propensity
to view you as a lumberjack,
a Northern bearded beauty
clad in plaid.

Oh how we loved when you kissed
with your eyes wide open
and your arms wrapped around us
in gentle muscular hugs.

No one worked a Pride Day wig
with such panache
and your stilettos
led to magical adventures.
Not even a broken heel
could stop you.

So many of us have met men
who could steal our hearts,
but so few like you
who'd give them back
improved.

Hopefully the beer is cold
and free, the sun hot
and your new world filled
with colourful wigs
large as weeping willows,
trees majestic in their ability
to bear great sadness
and fabulousness
all at once.

Polkaroo

In memory of Dennis Simpson, 1950–2010

I don't remember
whether I felt

innocent or experienced
kissing the star

of a favourite
childhood show

though I do remember
his entire body
danced

over me
and his tongue
conjured

rose petals
hummingbirds
imagination

Zaccheus

In memory of Zaccheus Nice Jackson, 1977–2014

I didn't know you well
but admired
the words

that shot
from your mouth
like firecrackers

exploding meaning
and wonder
over your audience.

Sometimes you'd scream to me
from your balcony
Nickerson! Nickerson!

and I'd look up
from Commercial Drive
where I'd swear

I could glimpse the lost
City of Atlantis
in the back of your throat.

Now that won't
happen again
and it guts me

the absence
echoing
with absence.

The world needs people
who scream names from balconies,
who acknowledge us

for no particular reason
other than
we're seen.

Your death is a tragedy!
So tragic Celine Dion
makes a cameo

and I'm sure
though you never liked Celine
you'd be totally stoked

to know she appears
in my poem
to you.

Zaccheus!
Zaccheus!
I scream your name.

Great Pyramids

At a writers' workshop on craft
Hiromi describes unconventional ways
characters can indicate time—

the stretches between haircuts,
menstrual cycles, how often
they clip their nails.

Children I babysat
understood their lives
by the number of sleeps

before big events,
and how many *Sesame Street*s
until their parents returned—

and my own body yearns
to acknowledge my life
outside the intervals

between lovers or dental appointments
until I remember the in-flight map
during a trip to Cairo

that helped me track our ETA
as twenty plays of the Bee Gees'
"How Deep Is Your Love"

and even though I would not recommend
listening to any song twenty times in a row
en route to Cairo

something about the mystical
nature of my destination
combined with the spectacle

of disco and brotherly harmonies
35,000 feet in the air
made it necessary

so in my seat
listening to the Bee Gees
I considered the depth

of my love
and all
I love and have loved

once then twice—
Robin and Maurice
backing up Barry

as if they haven't
already left this earth
—five times then six—

my first kiss, first boyfriend,
all those who've opened
or stolen or broken

my heart, all these
as the song progresses
—ten, eleven, twelve—

while flight attendants
confirm we've begun
our descent

and the song plays on
—eighteen, nineteen—
until we touch down

and a disco ball hangs
in the Great Pyramid
of my mind.

Love Coward or
What Happened after My Poem "Driving in
Adam's Jeep" Appeared on Poetry in Transit

For months I receive phone calls—
hey I'm in White Rock, hey I'm in Surrey,

hey I'm heading to school, I'm with my mom,
I'm just getting back from the doctor

and I saw your poem, I'm looking right at
your poem, OMG your poem, your poem

on the bus, on the Skytrain, on the B-line!
It's so amazing to see your words, your love

poem on the bus! How cool is that?
You've made it! You're for real!

I love how \\kiss me//
looks like windshield wipers!

I wish you could have kissed him.
I wanted him to kiss you—

and never for the rest of my life
will so many people read one of my poems,

a poem about wanting to kiss someone,
actually about wanting him to kiss me,

and sometimes I see my own poem,
sometimes it hovers over my head

while I commute from school
and lip-read people whispering my words.

One day a friend tells me he saw it
with the words LOVE COWARD

scrawled across it,
which is sorta true I guess

so at the very least I know
the vandal read the poem

but for how many weeks or months
was my poem read

with LOVE COWARD drawn
across it in dark marker,

how many nodding
in agreement?

Anonymous

Twenty years on and I still don't know
your name, what you do or who loves you
when we're not meeting each other
on streets lined with giant rainbows
and the possibility of sex.
Our time has been fraught
with quick embraces and frantic kisses,
intimate knowledge too often mistaken
for ownership.

There were times I wanted nothing other
than to ask your name, experience your life
outside our history of anonymity
and the hope that trust is built
on repetition.
I'm addicted to our narrative's plot:
each inciting incident, each rising action, each climax
and denouement of walking away.

I used to fear seeing you with your family
or someone you loved, fear sharing
more than a nod or a passing glance.
You wore hoodies first, then collared shirts
with neckties, then navy blue suits.
You've covered me with tattoos
I can only see with my eyes closed
or when I imagine your fingers.
We've grown middle-aged together
though every time I feel brand new.

How many times have we played this game—
hide-and-seek?
finders, keepers?
go, go, go, stop!?
Perhaps it's just a nameless thing
with few rules,
a maskless masquerade ball
we never stopped attending.

1.5 Times Normal

For Andreas

Learning to watch movies
at 1.5 times normal speed
is like watching stones skip across a lake.

The first few times
you can't quite isolate
each skip,

but eventually your mind
breaks down the blur
into discernible movements.

This leads me to question
pleasure and our capacity
to process small gestures

in a world prone to overlooking
nuance and meaning
at regular speed.

What about the characters
who already speak quickly

or zombies? Wouldn't quick zombies
seem like stupid humans?

Later that night when I kiss him
I'm determined
to make our moment last
as long as possible.

Skies

I'm four years old and pointing at an orange airplane in the sky. My father could be flying that plane and if I'm lucky he'll see me in our backyard. I jump up and down and wave my arms. I really want my dad to see me. If only I could jump just a little bit higher. If only I could wave faster, scream louder. I need to make him see.

My father flies 727s, an aircraft with three engines—one below each wing and one at the tail. It's iconic, but for much of my life an orange speck in the sky or what I shout about when a digital clock hits 7:27: "Daaaaaaad! It's 7:27! Daaaaaaad, it's your plane!"

* * *

Eileen Myles writes that unlike many friends who grew up in rural and suburban settings they spent most of their life in large American cities with a personal sky framed by immense skyscrapers. While I have seen skies composed by mountains, prairies, oceans and even the pyramids of Giza and the dancing Northern Lights, my personal sky is still the view from my childhood backyard in Langley, BC, where I'd gaze up past the clothesline connected to the large cedar, past its bird nests that some years were scavenged by raccoons, to where I'd look for my dad.

* * *

My dad rarely talks about how he began his flying career, though my mom would sometimes tell stories about how he cleaned the washrooms of the Moncton Flying Club to subsidize his flying lessons. She'd bring it up whenever she thought my gratitude needed a little adjusting or whenever I didn't work hard enough. *Your father used to scrub washroom floors with a toothbrush. You can mow the lawn.*

When he does talk about his early career it's always one of two stories. In the first he wears sunglasses just before nightfall, sunglasses he removes to squeeze out ten more minutes of daylight flying from his already adjusted eyes. The second involves his love of duct tape and how when bush piloting on Canada's east coast he'd sometimes use it to reinforce parts of his plane.

* * *

My father once brought me up to the cockpit. I didn't really care about the mechanics of flying or the speedometers or flight gauges. The cockpit window and the expansive view failed to elicit the magic I had always imagined from the ground. Like some hapless crow drunk on shininess, I pointed to the lights and colours: "What's that?"

It's a fuse, son.

"And that?"

A fuse.

"What about that?"

Another fuse.

It was our only time in the cockpit together.

* * *

Almost three decades later when I ask him about the early years of AIDS and its impact on his airline, *JeanEduardoPierreMarcTim* rolls off his tongue with a natural flow, like one long mellifluous name, a list of the flight attendants he worked with who died during the plague's first wave.

It strikes me as odd that my father had a more direct connection to the AIDS crisis in those first years than I did. We've never once talked about my gayness. When I came out on a Christmas Eve, he seemed nonchalant, as if it were intermittent turbulence.

We still love you, he said, and he has never mentioned it since.

* * *

It's the morning of September 11, 2001, and I'm walking into work at the UBC Bookstore I can tell something is wrong—the checkout area isn't filled with beginning-of-term crowds. What few customers and staff remain huddle around a cluster of televisions that usually play cheesy music videos. Today it broadcasts what seems a non-stop feed of the twin towers collapsing and then, as if by magic, reappearing only to meet the same Sisyphean fate.

My manager tells me planes have been hijacked in the skies all over North America. Worried about my father, I call home.

* * *

He flew for thirty-seven years. Apart from an emergency landing in Minnesota because a passenger slipped into cardiac arrest brought on by swallowing part of a broken swizzle stick, he had a safe, uneventful career. (The passenger survived. I still don't use swizzle sticks.) Of all those trips around the world, I worried more about his driving to and from the airports—especially after hearing how bandits in Lima, Peru, once stormed the airline crew bus and stole everyone's wallets, jewellery and shoes. *Even their shoes*, he'd say.

* * *

I love when airplanes tow banners across the sky: *Gina, will you marry me? Have you tried our new pizza crust? Hug somebody you love.* No matter how commercial or clichéd, those messages make me smile. Though I know it's not him piloting, it's as if he's up there. I feel the same about words scrolling along electronic billboards or when aerobatic teams draw giant smoky hearts.

* * *

Things my father brought me from his trips: fake Benetton shirts from Bangkok, Hawaiian macadamia nuts, black licorice and a book about the Anne Frank Museum from Amsterdam, saltwater taffy from Halifax, French-language newspapers I struggled to understand, bootleg DVDs from Asia, coins from around the world and a miniature boomerang from Australia I was forbidden to use.

Some nights I'd fantasize about taking it down from my bedroom wall and sneaking into my backyard to perfect my throw. I can still hear the soundtrack from those fantasies: whoosh and whoosh and whoosh until, somehow, it would appear in my hand.

* * *

My father is at home dying from an esophageal tumour. He is one of many pilots of his generation afflicted by upper-torso cancers. Some blame radiation and the first jetliners' thin skins, but studies have proven inconclusive and the only evidence remains the names of fallen pilots. I can't help but think it's unfair he's stuck here on the ground. Can't help but think of Icarus and the sun. Can't help.

* * *

My father never acted like the pilots I'd see on TV. Apart from the requisite moustache, he didn't live a macho lifestyle of womanizing and big spending. He'd often eat at cheap diners so he could save his per diems to pay for a family vacation to Disneyland.

On one trip, Dad and I rode a roller coaster that clanked its way to the summit, but instead of plunging down the slope, I felt as though my body was in our backyard again, waving at us as we flew across the sky.

A Baker's Dozen

13 Vancouver Food (in)Securities

1.

When the old Italians
drape their fig trees
in mesh nets
to keep out the birds
it seems as if the trees
are walking home
from the salon.

2.

My favourite blackberry bushes
were cleared out
to stop the homeless.

In their place now stands
a condo complex
few of us can afford.

3.

At my local café
a customer admits
he's never considered
food security before,
but now might need
to buy a lock
for his refrigerator.
I sip my coffee,
burn my tongue.

4.

Sometimes I purchase ginger snaps
from Uprising Breads Bakery
where my friend was a manager
before his death.
Each morsel a memorial.

5.

There's a store in Kitsilano
where organic jelly beans
retail for $25 a kilogram.
Unlike in *Jack and the Beanstalk*,
these beans are not magic,
just expensive.
There are no golden eggs.

6.

Inside the cheap pizza place
customers debate
the merits of pineapple

while outside someone tries
to panhandle enough
for a slice.

7.

Gelato stores are the cockroaches
of the hospitality world.
No matter how often
or by how much rent increases,
somehow they survive.

8.

Small bones litter the ground
under the bald eagles' nest
in the park
among the advisory signs:
Watch out
for poisoned sausages.

9.

My friend stipulates
for her birthday meal
that everyone shares.
None of this ordering
for yourself crap.

10.

Rat-proof.
Crow-proof.
Raccoon-proof.
Dog-proof.
Bear-proof.
Human-proof.
The ultimate
dumpster.

11.

Minimum wage,
maximum rage.

12.

The restaurant offering
pay-what-you-can
closed down
after the landlord offered
pay-what-you-can't.

13.

At the First Nations Restaurant
at the Folklife pavilion
during Expo 86
I overhear a tourist
ask a busser
What did your people drink?

Um, probably just water
the young man answers,
which disappoints her.

Langley

After Joe Brainard

I remember walking under the power lines near my house and how if it was raining and you held an umbrella you'd sometimes get a shock.

I remember trapping grasshoppers in ice cream pails and pickle jars, learning the hard way to poke holes in the lids.

I remember neighbourhood kids throwing their pennies into my Mr. Turtle Pool after I convinced them it doubled as a wishing well,

the u-pick strawberry patch that closed down as deer liked strawberries too

and thinking the first condom I saw on the nearby nature trails was a deflated balloon.

I remember my school was named after long-time Langley educator Alice Brown, though I wished it had been named after Laura Secord, like the one in Vancouver, as I believed students there received free chocolate.

I remember the school secretary, Mrs. Montgomery, would use the same structure for all her announcements—*Mr. Jones to the office, please, Mr. Jones*—and how we'd mimic her during recess and lunch— *Jason, what's in your lunch today, Jason?*

I remember Shane Stackhouse and all the other Jehovah's Witnesses in the hallway each morning during the Lord's Prayer and holiday craft sessions,

and that Mr. Shipley, my PE teacher, married Miss Ross, who taught me choir, during the summer, and her new name confused everyone when we returned in the fall.

I remember my school divided into house teams—Haida, Nootka, Salish, Bella Coola—though nobody ever taught us the names' true origins, so when I hear them I first think of my school.

I remember Jasvinder preferred to be called Vinder as he thought it sounded cool like Darth Vader. Every other Jasvinder I've met has preferred to go by Jas.

I remember finding out that the Great Wall Restaurant where my family ate buffet referred to the Great Wall of China and had nothing to do with the great wall of buffet items,

and buying Mexican jumping beans, smashing one with a hammer to reveal a small worm, then trying to replace that worm's home with a bottle cap of water and a clump of grass in a pickle jar.

I remember a lot of pickle jars though surprisingly few pickles.

I remember my dad refused to let my mom put coins in my birthday cake as he worried we'd get sued if one of my friends choked to death,

and thinking the yellow shell on the Shell oil sign was a giant piece of cheese, then marvelling that the giant piece of cheese was shaped like a shell.

I remember my parents ordering pizzas and having me sit by the front window to wait for the pizzas the very moment they were ordered, even though it would take at least 30 minutes for them to arrive—

and the time the pizza man forgot to put his car in park, so after he opened his door the car rolled backwards and the pizza boxes slipped from his hand onto the asphalt, where the tire rolled over them.

The pizza man ran over our pizzas! The pizza man ran over our pizzas! I screamed, but no one believed me until a meek teenager knocked on our door and said, *I'm sorry, sir, but I seem to have run over your pizzas.*

I remember my father calling the pizza place to tell them their driver ran over our pizzas, and they thought it was a prank call and hung up.

I remember my local MP, Bob Wenman, awarding me a Canadian flag pin at my school assembly after I was the only student in kindergarten who could name our prime minister, Pierre Trudeau—

and the immediate silence of the drunk teenagers in the back seat of the car driven by that same MP in the McDonald's drive-thru I later worked at when I said *Hey, aren't you Bob Wenman?*

I remember microwaving Cheez Whiz to make quick nachos, burning the roof of my mouth almost as badly as when I'd drink vending-machine hot chocolate.

I remember the Avon lady, who I called to buy my mom a Christmas present of snowman-shaped soaps, who referred to her husband as "the husband" and whose husband always r eferred to her as "the wife."

I remember when Scott and Danny's parents divorced.
I remember when Melanie and Kim's parents divorced.
I remember when Erin and Davy's parents divorced.
I remember when Darren and Adam's parents divorced.

I remember Mike Reno, the lead singer of Loverboy, visited my elementary school and signed one kid's arm with a felt pen and how that kid screamed *I'm never washing my arm again!* but he did eventually (I checked his arm each day).

I remember learning about menstruation from Brooke Shields in
The Blue Lagoon

and how when my aunt Susan picked me up from school hours after
learning she was pregnant, she repeated *Twins, twins! I'm pregnant
with twins!* the entire drive home.

I remember being called a frog because I was in French immersion,
a preppy because I wore dress shoes, and a faggot because that's
what happened when pickup trucks with rolled-down windows
drove past.

I remember my mom changed our rescue dog's name from Misty to
Mitsy—it was easier to say with my lisp.

I remember finding out about my friend Karie's death from the front
page of the *Langley Times*. I thought the prayer stools at her Catholic
funeral were footrests.

I remember having to take off my shoes before eating at the Okinawa
Garden restaurant and how my parents' drinks were served in small
statues of geishas and warriors that could be taken home and used
to hold pens or cut flowers.

I remember my mom's embarrassment at having to tell me it was
Gladys Knight and the Pips, not Gladys Knight and the Pimps,

and renting violent movies from the Blockbuster Video where I
worked to the husband I'd later learn beat my mom's friend.

I remember Mrs. Gray, the school librarian, reading Dennis Lee's
Garbage Delight. I loved when Suzie grew a moustache and Polly
grew a beard.

I remember *Ramona the Brave*, *The Lion, the Witch and the Wardrobe* and Judy Blume's *Superfudge*.

I remember my friends Carmen Porter and Christie Brown loved only horses, and then they loved only horses and Shaun Cassidy, and then they loved only Shaun Cassidy.

I remember the birdhouse my dad hung high in the backyard cedar after a nest fell from the tree during a storm.

I remember my whole family standing around that nest, and the shock when I saw that the eggs inside were the same colour as the sky.

Curiosa

V4G 1N4

If you search
V4G 1N4
on Google Maps,

you'll discover
it's in Delta, BC—
a city named

for the triangular
tract of land
at the river's mouth.

You don't have to be
a delta lover
to appreciate this,

nor should you ignore
the beauty
of the red spot

that identifies the pleasure
of arriving
at your destination.

I've Got a Secret

A few weeks ago I received an email
inviting me to take part in a special event
organized by *Sad Magazine*,
whose publishers are generally happy people.
The email requested I write a poem
for a poetry and comedy showcase,
which is a little like hosting
a showcase of sandpaper and hand jobs,
but I'm not one to shy away
from difficult or awkward situations.
Why the fuck not? I told myself
and emailed them
with a thank-you.
Poetry and comedy it would be—
especially given that I misread the email
so instead of the evening's theme, *secrets*,
I somehow got it into my head
we were to write about "secretions"
and spent the next three weeks
reliving and itemizing
all I could remember
oozing from my body.
I can't say I'm a big fan
of everything I've produced,
but I much prefer it
when I have an idea
of its origins.
During an X-ray for a severely twisted ankle,
my friend's technician asked her
if she was there because of the needle
lodged in her foot—
What needle? she asked
but in the X-ray

could see the outline of its small eye
and realized she stood on a needle
that had remained inside her
for god knows how many years.
A nurse friend once encountered
a patient who calmly explained
he'd inserted an AA battery
into his urethra
and couldn't get it out,
but unlike my friend and her foot needle
I'm pretty sure he remembers it
sliding inside him,
not to mention the dreadful
revelation he hadn't purchased
the AAAs he'd intended to.

But my poem needed to address
what has left my body,
not internal discoveries,
so I spent weeks thinking about
my fluids and the rainbow
of colours I've produced—
kinda like the love child
between Roy G. Biv and STI—
and how some of the fluids
were someone else's—
like the drummer from Spinal Tap
who choked to death on vomit,
only it wasn't his own vomit—
but by that time I had learned
the night's true theme
so I didn't need to share
my detailed list,
which is probably for the better.

Ball Twins

I sometimes wonder if penises
are like snowflakes
in that no two penises
are exactly the same.

That can't be said
about balls though,
as I once met a man
who had my identical balls,

which made us uncomfortable
until we realized
they must have been quadruplets
separated at birth.

Now our balls call
on Christmas and birthdays,
correspond via snail mail
like pen pals.

This past Valentine's Day,
my balls received a card
on which a jubilant squirrel exclaims
I'm nuts about you!

Let Them Eat Snake

At the farmers' market a couple debates
whether their kids should be allowed

to order snake burgers
at the exotic meats tent.

She thinks it's wonderful
her kids want to explore,

but he questions the ethics
of snake eating,

whether it's worth the expense
versus other local options.

I know I shouldn't get involved
but I can't help myself

so I blurt out
Just give them hot dogs

and say it's snake,
they won't know the difference,

but this doesn't go over well
with the couple, who immediately hug

as though there's been an earthquake,
some violent act of God.

To Friends Who've Worked in Porn

For Adam Avery

When people at parties
ask the name of the street

on which you grew up
or the name of your first pet

I guess it's best
to play along

as nobody wants to be a killjoy
or that person

who helpfully offers that
sharing your mother's maiden name

is a surefire path
to identity theft.

Plenty of identities
are stolen every day,

just not in the way
people assume they are.

Hashtags

used to be
the scars
on your chin
from hot knifing.

Think of all that
aloe vera
and how quickly
things change.

The Taxidermist

cried on national television
when a reporter asked
how his family
will cope
with the flood

and I couldn't stop
thinking about those animals,
whether they'd be mourned
a second time.

Sea Turtles

Some sea turtles
can't keep afloat
due to the weight

of barnacles
clinging
to their shells.

I wonder if it's only
barnacles
weighing them down.

Perhaps I'm projecting
my burdens again,
anthropomorphizing

turtle dilemmas,
turtle dreams,
rough seas.

Surrealism

I wonder how many teachers
have used Dali's lobster phone
to explain surrealism.

At some point what's irrational
will cease to be the lobster,
become the clunky phone.

How to Clean a Gravestone

Create a small tent
over the gravestone.

Use polyethylene
to cover the stone

and pieces of wood
to keep it grounded.

You can find snails
on the surrounding graves.

Collect and place them
in the enclosure.

Make sure to poke
holes for ventilation.

Check back after a few hours.
If they were hungry

the stone will be
pretty clean.

Acknowledgements

This manuscript was compiled and often written on the unceded and ancestral lands of the Musqueam, Squamish, Stó:lo and Tsleil-Waututh peoples.

Thank you to Karen Solie for sharing her poetic eye and surprising knowledge of popular culture, and to the many friends who gave feedback on these poems.

Thank you also to Jay and Hazel Millar and all the folks at Book*hug for fighting the good fight, and to Stuart Ross for his copy-editing prowess.

Thank you to the following journals and their editors for publishing earlier versions of the following poems:

Arc—"1.5 Times Normal"
CV2—"Six Years On"
The Fiddlehead—"Pickle Farmer"
Geist—"Kissing in New Zealand" and "V4G 1N4"
Malahat Review—"Skies"
Oratorealis—"Zaccheus"
Prism International—"Pretty in Love" and "Ball Twins"
Rusty Toque—"Leather Bar"

"A Bakers Dozen: 13 Food (in)Securities" appeared in *Sustenance: Writers from BC and Beyond on the Subject of Food* (ed. Rachel Rose, Anvil Press).

"Langley" was presented as part of a keynote presentation at the 2018 Fraser Valley Literary Festival in Abbotsford, BC.

The cabeza of "Pretty in Love" is from the song "The Power of Love" by Frankie Goes to Hollywood.

"Hiromi" in the poem "Great Pyramids" refers to the wonderful writer Hiromi Goto.

"How to Clean a Gravestone" is a found poem taken from wikihow.com/Clean-a-Gravestone.

Thank you to Kwantlen Polytechnic University for granting me an educational leave and to the Kuldip Gill Fellowship residency at University of the Fraser Valley, during which some of these poems were written.

About the Author

Billeh Nickerson is the author of six books, including *Artificial Cherry*, which was nominated for the City of Vancouver Book Award. He a past Editor of both Event and Prism International, and co-editor of the groundbreaking anthology *Seminal: The Anthology of Canada's Gay Male Poets*. He lives and works in Vancouver where he is the co-chair of the Creative Writing department at Kwantlen Polytechnic University.

Colophon

Manufactured as the first edition of
Duct-Taped Roses
in the spring of 2021 by Book*hug Press

Edited for the press by Karen Solie
Copy edited by Stuart Ross

Cover photo-illustration: Lind Design and iStock/ozgurdonmaz
Design and typesetting: Lind Design
Type: Mrs Eaves, Mr Eaves, Campione Neue Sans and Gelato Script